INDUSTRIAL REVOLUTION

THE RISE OF THE MACHINES (TECHNOLOGY AND INVENTIONS)

History Book 6th Grade

Children's History

In this book, we're going to talk about the Industrial Revolution. So, let's get right to it!

WHAT WAS THE INDUSTRIAL REVOLUTION?

The Industrial Revolution was a huge change in the way that people created products. Before the Industrial Revolution most people made their goods in their home by hand or in small shops. For example, if you wanted to make cloth, you might grow the materials on a farm, then create the threads, and then weave the threads together to make a fabric. Finally, after you created the fabric, you would have to cut it and then stitch it together to make a piece of clothing. It was a very labor-intensive process and it was done this way for thousands of years.

ABACA FIBER

TEXTILE MACHINES
41
WOOD WOR MILLS

The Industrial Revolution was a time when new technologies and inventions were introduced that made it possible for people to create products much faster than before. These new machines were placed in large factories and people moved from farms to cities to take these jobs. There were also many new innovations in transportation, which made it possible for both people and goods to get to their destinations faster.

WHERE DID THE INDUSTRIAL REVOLUTION START?

Great Britain was the first country to experience the Industrial Revolution. It started in the last part of the 1700s. Some of the first new technologies began with the way that textiles were produced. Instead of making cloth at home, the production of cloth began to move to factories. The country had plenty of fuel in the form of coal, which was needed to make the machines in the factories run.

MACHINES MAKING COTTON THREAD

HOW LONG DID THE INDUSTRIAL REVOLUTION LAST?

The transition to this new way to produce products lasted for the span of about a century. After its start in Great Britain, the wave of changes spread to other countries in Europe and then across the Atlantic Ocean to the United States. The transition to the industrial economy took place in two different phases.

INDUSTRIAL REVOLUTION PHASE ONE

This first part of the Industrial Revolution began toward the end of the 1700s. The move from homes to factories for the production of textiles was its start. Using steam to power engines was an important innovation during this part of the Industrial Revolution. The cotton gin, which was a machine used to separate the fibers of cotton and its seeds, was an important new invention during this time period as well. This phase ended in the middle of the 1800s.

COTTON GIN

BESSEMER FURNACE

INDUSTRIAL REVOLUTION PHASE TWO

The next phase began in the middle of the 1800s and continued into the early part of the 1900s. New inventions made it possible for mass production of goods. Electrical power to run machines and factory production lines were important new technologies. The Bessemer process for the production of steel was important as well.

WHEN DID THE INDUSTRIAL REVOLUTION START IN THE UNITED STATES?

The Industrial Revolution began in the United States in the year 1793. That was the year that Samuel Slater opened a textile mill in Rhode Island. He had learned his craft in England and brought his mastery of the trade to the US. The Industrial Revolution spread from the northeast across the country and by the last part of the 1800s, the United States was more industrial than any other nation worldwide.

TEXTILE MILL

WHAT CULTURAL CHANGES HAPPENED DURING THE INDUSTRIAL REVOLUTION?

The life of the everyday person changed radically during the Industrial Revolution. Instead of a quiet, hard-working country life, people moved to crowded cities to work. They sometimes had to live in noisy, squalid, unsanitary conditions. The air was polluted from the burning of coal and it was a different pace of life than farm living had been. People who were used to open air and lots of space were now living in tight, crowded quarters.

WHAT WERE WORKING CONDITIONS LIKE DURING THE INDUSTRIAL REVOLUTION?

There were many good things about the changes created by the Industrial Revolution, but one of its disadvantages was the working conditions in factories. At that time, there were very few regulations or laws designed to protect workers. The new machines they were using as well as other conditions in the mills and factories were frequently dangerous. However, by the last part of the 1900s, this changed largely due to labor unions that pushed for safer conditions for workers.

LARGE, HEAVY, STEEL MACHINERY

Everything changed in a short period of time during the Industrial Revolution. There were new power sources, new ways to get from place to place, and new ways to communicate.

During the first part of the Industrial Revolution, the new machines needed water power or wind power to operate. However, soon the power of steam was introduced and ways to distribute electricity to homes and factories changed the way machines could be powered. These innovations made the Industrial Revolution advance.

OLD VINTAGE STEAM MACHINERY

INDUSTRIAL MACHINES

STEAM ENGINES

Although people had used the power of steam for a while, there wasn't a practical way to use it to operate machinery until James Watt invented an engine powered by steam in 1781. This engine could be used to run factory machines. Because of this innovation, factories didn't need to be located where there was water or wind power available.

As the 1800s progressed, engines run by steam got larger and they were able to power more and more. They were used to give power to machines in factories and they were also used for steamboats and steam locomotives.

PESO REALE   t. 86
PESO FRENATO t. 89
DEP. LOC. BOLOGNA C.LE
90 83 2525 100-1 T

ELECTRICITY

During the second phase of the Industrial Revolution, electrical power was used to light up factories and other buildings. From the end of the 1800s forward, lights powered by electricity made it possible for factories to run longer shifts of work into the evening and night.

The first practical light bulb was created by American
inventor Thomas Edison in 1879.

WEAVING AND WARPING

TECHNOLOGY FOR TEXTILES

The textile industry had huge changes and growth during the Industrial Revolution. This was due to many new inventions. Four of the most important inventions were the spinning jenny, the spinning mule, the cotton gin, and the sewing machine.

THE SPINNING JENNY

The spinning jenny was invented in 1764 by James Hargreaves. A regular spinning wheel could only spin one thread of cotton yarn at a time. However, the spinning jenny made it possible for the operator to turn one wheel and spin eight times that amount of thread all at the same time.

MULE-SPINNING ROOM

THE SPINNING MULE

Samuel Crompton improved the spinning mule in 1779. This machine was designed to manufacture threads of high quality. One operator could control 1,000 spindles at the same time. The machine was capable of producing fine or course yarns. It was called a mule because it was a combination of two different inventions, just like a mule is the offspring of a male donkey and a female horse.

THE COTTON GIN

In 1793, the cotton gin was invented by Eli Whitney. This allowed the seeds of the cotton plant to be removed by machine instead of by hand. Cotton production became highly profitable in the United States and unfortunately meant that more slaves were used to pick cotton in the fields.

MEN WORKING IN A COTTON GIN

SEWING MACHINE

THE SEWING MACHINE

In 1846, the sewing machine was invented by Elias Howe. This machine allowed seamstresses to sew clothing much faster than hand stitching. It was eventually improved by Isaac Singer who started the Singer Sewing Machine Company.

Hargreaves and Crompton were British inventors and Whitney, Howe, and Singer were Americans.

TRANSPORTATION

The textile industry wasn't the only industry that had rapid change during the Industrial Revolution. Transportation made a huge leap forward during this era.

The improved production of goods meant items had to be transported faster so they could be sold in both urban and country areas. Robert Fulton, an American inventor, created the first practical steamboat. It was quickly used to carry products and passengers up and down rivers in the US.

STEAMBOAT

525 100

The beginning of the 1800s saw the first steam locomotives. Trains became a very important form of transportation during this era. Soon railways were built all over Britain and other countries in Europe.

In the United States, the First Transcontinental Railroad was finished in 1869, allowing goods and passengers to go from the east coast to the west coast.

TELEGRAPH

COMMUNICATION

The telegraph and then the telephone revolutionized communication during the 1800s. Samuel Morse, an American inventor, invented the telegraph, which was run by electricity, in 1844. It allowed messages to be transmitted much more quickly than messages carried by horse.

The Scottish-born inventor, Alexander Graham Bell, created the first practical telephone in 1876. It changed the speed of communication forever.

INDUSTRIAL REVOLUTION AND ITS CONTRIBUTION TO MODERNIZATION

The Industrial Revolution completely transformed the economies of Europe and the United States. There were huge innovations in the textile industry, the transportation industry, and the communications industry. People moved from the country to the city so they could take jobs in factories.

Awesome! Now that you've read about the Industrial Revolution, you may want to read more about the simple machines people used before the Industrial Revolution in the Baby Professor book Simple Machines: The Way They Work – Physics Books for Kids.

Visit
BABY PROFESSOR
EDUCATION KIDS
www.BabyProfessorBooks.com
to download Free Baby Professor eBooks
and view our catalog of new and exciting
Children's Books

9 7 9 8 8 6 9 4 3 4 9 6 8